MW00711943

THE SECRET OF WORKING KNOWINGLY WITH GOD

*Adapted from a talk given by
Walter Russell in 1946*

The University of Science and Philosophy
P.O. Box 520
Waynesboro, Virginia 22980
www.philosophy.org

The Secret of Working Knowingly With God
by Walter Russell
(1871 - 1963)

Copyright 1993 by
The University of Science and Philosophy
Second Printing 2008

ISBN 978-1-879605-38-1

Edited by Emilia Lee Lombardi
Cover design by Erin Rachel Hudak
Printed by Mid Valley Press

The quality and pattern of your outgivings will crystallize into body form in the image of your thinking. That is

LAW

What you give out will return to you in your image.

ALL KNOWLEDGE
EXISTETH

"All knowledge cometh to man in its season.

Cosmic messengers periodically give to man such knowledge of My cosmos as man is able to comprehend,

but

that which he can bear is like unto a thimbleful out of the mighty ocean, for man is but beginning to comprehend."

–The Divine Iliad

THE SECRET OF WORKING KNOWINGLY WITH GOD

By Walter Russell

This is a purposeful talk in an endeavor to give you a better comprehension of the relationship of man to his universe and to his God. Its ultimate purpose is to uplift the individual to a higher Being, and by uplifting the individual we uplift the entire human race one notch higher.

The thing that holds man back is his disbelieving, his doubting, and especially his lack of comprehension. *Everyone is absolutely dependent on God at every moment. We can do nothing without Him, and you might as well know it. And the more you do know it, the more power comes to you to manifest God.*

I am, however, a bit reluctant to give this talk because of the personal equation which comes into it. I very much dislike the necessity of using the personal pronoun "I," but so many people have asked me specifically and with great sincerity to tell them how it is possible to acquire a complete education from the cosmos, from the invisible universe. They are so mystified by it that I think you are entitled to as good a dissertation upon the subject as I can give you.

Tonight's talk is that of a life, my own life. It should uplift and inspire you to greater and higher things, and in that sense I am glad to give it. The reason I can tell this is that I have lived it, and because I have lived it the proof should be believed because the evidence is there. Otherwise you wouldn't be here and Glenn Clark would not have written his little book.*

*The Man Who Tapped The Secrets of The Universe, University of Science and Philosophy, Swannanoa, Waynesboro, Virginia.

I am also often asked: "What have you got that I haven't got? Why is it that I cannot do those things which you can do?"

My only answer is: You have what I have. We *all* have it. But one is aware of it and the other is not. One works toward the body, the other toward the Spirit. All of my life I have been working toward the Spirit with God, *knowingly*, and the proof of it is there.

We Start At The Beginning

I am going to start right back at the very beginning, at seven years of age, when something tremendous happened to me, something indescribable, something so beautiful, so wonderful, a sort of complete blotting out of everything concerning the physical universe, concerning my body. A great burst of changing, changing colors — blue, violet, orange — seemed to fill and pervade all space and me. I was swallowed up in it. Then that ceased and there was a blinding flash and I stood motionless. I had been playing marbles with other boys and was holding marbles in my hand. Instead of tossing them, I walked away.

I realized that *something* had happened but I couldn't tell what it was. Within me was a vibration of such exquisite rhythm and harmony, such beauty and ecstasy, that I thought something had descended from the heavens— and it had. For a long time I wandered in the fields. I climbed up into an apple tree, and sat there for a long, long time. Then I went home and tried to get my mother to explain what had happened to me. I told her all about it and she said, "Well, if you're not all right tomorrow I'll take you to a doctor." Tomorrow I was all right so she did not take me to a doctor.

The effect of that experience lasted for days. I was then seven years of age; I had started school at five. Now I found that I could not go to school. I did go as I should but I just couldn't stay there; I couldn't stand it. I couldn't open books and look at them. So I wandered. That lasted for days.

I felt that I was a different being; that I was something else than I had ever known before. I wish I could describe it to you. I had my first glimpse of that "other universe," that which we call the *conscious* universe but I prefer to call it the *knowing* universe because it is the beginning and the end. It is the foundation of all our power, our knowledge, and our life. I had been living in the *knowing* universe but was not aware of it.

I Found Myself Doing Extraordinary Things

Then it all passed. I found myself doing extraordinary things. I was playing the piano very well at that age but found I could play much better, astonishingly better. Everybody noticed it. As I practiced, I found that there was *something* inside of me seemingly talking to me and telling me that God was working with me, not the God-nature in me but the *Supreme Force.* That was something that I didn't understand at the time and couldn't call "God," but there was some unknown tremendous *Force* telling me, when I touched the keys on the piano, for instance, to do something else rather than what I was used to doing before. There was more music in my playing, more Soul in it, more beauty and more skill. It seemed that I had doubled my power of expressing myself in music almost overnight.

I went back to school after that wore away but found that I couldn't open books anymore. There seemed to be something like a hand or a wall put up that kept me from opening books. And if I opened them *I had to close them* because I had become aware that what was in those books was either of no importance or it wasn't so. And if they were on mathematics or grammar, or anything of that nature, that I did not need to know it now. In fact, all I could do in school was to sit there.

I was judged dumb. I was the bright boy of the class who had suddenly turned dumb. I failed in mathematics; I failed in everything. But I could do whatever required *knowledge and inspiration.* I amazed people with what I did along those lines. I amazed people when they asked me and I answered them.

What I Wished To Know, I Knew

Time went on and another May came and it happened again, but not as prolonged this time. It happened again the following May, but also not as prolonged—but enough, however, to make me aware that there was something happening to prepare me for a different kind of life.

I was taken out of school and put to work. I'm very, very thankful for that because I did not like school after the age of seven. It was very different and very unpleasant — and it seemed to me to be very unnecessary. What I wished to know, I knew. What I desired to do, I asked that I might do *and started doing it with the utmost conviction that I could do it.*

At ten and eleven and twelve years of age, it happened again. At thirteen it happened again, more and more. Every year in May, from ten to fourteen days, I would always have to go into the woods, go somewhere away from people.

It was noticed, yes. My mother called it "his queer spells, and he always gets over them." So they didn't worry.

By the time I reached fourteen, twice seven, I knew there was a deep purpose in life for me. I was commanded to demonstrate power— to demonstrate power that was drawn from a *Source* that was *within me* rather than from a source outside of me.

Then I "Died"

Then I had one of the most dreadful diseases that could afflict humankind, the bubonic plague. It was called black diphtheria. Doctors had taken cultures from my throat which were blacker than a case knife. Black diphtheria had destroyed my throat and shut off my breathing. And then I "died." I was pronounced dead by one doctor. Two others were called in and they pronounced me dead, also. They sent for the undertaker. The undertaker had arrived. The soul does not leave the body right away, the consciousness does not. The awareness of the purpose that I must fulfill gave me knowledge of the healing principle right then and there, and I was commanded that I should use it upon myself. I did, and once again I was strongly alive in the body. I arose from that bed and I was well.

The doctors were amazed. My father was sitting by the bedside weeping. I couldn't gather my senses all at once and I wondered why he was weeping. I said, "Don't cry, father, I'll put that coal in." The last thing I remembered before I became ill was that I was supposed to put a ton of coal in through the cellar window. Everyone was amazed. "I'm not dead," I said. "I'm thoroughly well."

They sent for some other doctors and they, too, were astounded. It didn't seem possible; it could not be. They all talked so much about it, saying that it just couldn't be, that the thing called "fear" got into me and I then wondered about it myself. So many things were said that this "fear," even though a little bit of it, gave me total paralysis of my body from head to toe. It took fully six months to pass away. *I had that paralysis of my body due simply to the fact that the doctors were saying things that aroused doubts and fears in me that I was even alive!*

That was when I was fourteen — twice seven. Every May after that it happened again and again. And always I did things that I could never have done before.

I always wandered in the woods and sought the intense ecstatic joy of the Soul with the consciousness stepping in and out of the body, *in and out of the body.* That is the only way I can express it to you.

I Was Impelled To Write Things

I want you to know what I mean by that by reading several pages from what I later called *The Book of Early Whisperings* for always in that state I was impelled to write things. During those ten days or so, I was impelled to write my impressions and lock them up. No one had ever seen them. Some instinct told me to lock them up and keep them. *The Book of Early Whisperings* is the junior edition of *The Divine Iliad* which came later, and that also was locked up in the same way.

In 1921, I found out why I had to lock them up, because I was made fully aware of my purpose and those things were not to appear until after 1946.

I am going to read a section from *The Book of Early Whisperings.* Before I do so, however,

I want to tell you <u>why</u> I am doing it. It is to make you aware that when you are fully conscious of God in you and God working with you *knowingly,* you cannot produce anything which is <u>not</u> enduring art. You produce perfection; you produce consummate art. It couldn't be otherwise. What I am now reading to you I wrote at the age of nineteen. I had never written anything before, and yet when some of the doctors later, in 1921, were examining me to see if I were really out of my mind or not, they came across some of these writings. There was a doctor, a lawyer and an alienist, and one of them said to my wife, "Leave him alone. There's something happening to him that we don't understand. An insane man is not logical; he couldn't be logical. These writings out-Whitman Walt Whitman. They are not only logical but they are beautiful poetic art, perfect literature."

I had never studied literature or literary form. Since nine-and-a-half I had not even been to school. As I read this to you, I want you to feel the *stepping in and out of the body* into the observation of physical phenomena. Up until then, nothing of this sort could even be known, that of being within the body for a moment and then fully out of it.

The Awakening

I breathe the air from the hills. The strength of the hills is in me. It courses through my veins. It comes to me from the mountain tops beyond the hills, where the eye within me is fixed.

It is Light. I feel it ever coming. I take it into me. I feel the strength of the Light that I am taking into me.

I smell the sweet odor and I drink in the sunshine. I open my lungs to the forest. I draw strength from a super-power which is Light.

I am that Power. It is all of me. I am all of it.

With my feet firmly planted to earth I tear trees from their roots and dash them aside. It is nothing for me to tear trees from the earth tree by tree or forest by forest.

My strength transcends that of the tree. It is mightier than that of the forest.

The strength of all of the forests and all of the hills is in me. The earth lends me its power. The winds lend me their power.

The winds of the earth are my breath. I breathe and forests rise and fall.

With the deer I run and leap, but they are motionless when I run with them. With the bird I fly and more effectually.

Sitting by the pathside I need but to think of there and I am there, or some other where. And in another breath I am back again.

For the deer is a deer and the bird is a bird; but I am a man with a Soul; a man with an uncaged Soul.

I wander with my Self in my world, my body awandering with my Soul, companions for just a little while; then my Soul wanders alone.

My body is but the house of my Soul; its carriage; the roots which tie it to earth when it will be tied. It is not me. I am sure of that. I have long known that.

Some day I'll write down what I know of it; and what each new moment whispers to me of it; and the silences. What the silences say of it I will write down some day, if I ever can.

Little things call my Soul back from afar; little things; the curve of a sapling; the shadow of a cloud over a meadow. And the same little things send it awandering back again into space while my body awaits it on the path, or goes to meet it, absently, all unconscious of its movement; like a dead leaf on a flowing stream.

The spirit of Beauty balances my Soul as a well of running water replenishes the earth.

I seek Beauty in the far spaces of my wandering and find it when thus awandering. Always I find it when my weightless Soul extends within the extensions of the stars and leaves the house of clay which binds it to the mountain side.

Rains replenish the well as Beauty replenishes my Soul. Without the Beauty of the great out-of-doors I feel that my body would become too parched and dry to long be companion to my Soul.

There is a brook to the right. The water falls over the rock into the limpid pool. I go eagerly to see it. The water drops over in the shadow of a great rock patined with lichens—like a bronze patined by rain.

The sun peeps into the pool and some very yellow leaves capture its rays to herald its coming.

The green moss is velvet; the softest of velvet.

Wintergreen are there awaiting me, and checker-ferns. Arbutus leaves cover a bit of turf; its pink blossoms sing their spring-song.

Pulpit-Jacks show me their zebra stripings, modestly.

The shadow of a leaf falls upon another leaf; and still another leaf silhouettes itself upon a rock.

Quite unaware of me a busy ant makes its way across the rock carrying something much larger than itself.

I am as certain that I am that ant as that I am I. I carry that burden with the ant. I feel my body straining with that burden of the ant.

I am alone with all this activity. Shall I turn to the right or to the left?

What matters it? Even now I feel my Soul parting from its anchorage of heavy clay. I see my Light interwoven with the Universal Light..

From: *The Book of Early Whisperings*

That is the essence of my boyhood. That beautiful spiritual foundation is the rock upon which I built my life. The desire to do wonderful and beautiful things to interpret the rhythms of Nature was strong in me. I expressed it in painting; I expressed it in these writings, many,

many of them, a goodly sized volume of them which will come out some day not too far in the future. I also expressed it in my music.

I expressed power as well as great art. I had it thoroughly in my consciousness that there was nothing I should do that was not masterly. Do you see that line, *"It is nothing for me to tear trees from the earth tree by tree or forest by forest"?* That is the impression that I always had, that there was nothing I could not do. Tearing trees or forests apart by their roots was merely a symbol of the power I felt at all times. If I ever desired to do a thing, no matter what that thing was, I did it. I always felt God in me. I felt God sitting beside me at the piano or within me, making me do much more than I ever could have done before, and in less time.

Knowledge Belongs To The
Spiritual Universe

I found myself getting more and more acquainted with the *"knowing"* universe and beginning to *know* rather than to think. I began to segregate knowledge from information and knowledge from thinking. Thinking is taking knowledge apart and setting it in motion. *Thinking belongs to the electric universe; knowledge belongs to the spiritual universe.*

I spent my hours and days and leisure moments in *knowing*. The invisible universe became mine. Every seven years this experience happened increasingly more, and every seventh year I did more amazing things.

It was during one of those periods that I started designing buildings because the artists needed buildings for their studios. I knew nothing about architecture. I opened an architect's office, employed engineers, and designed buildings upon a new plan that you may have read about in that little book, so I won't waste time talking about it now. It was a new plan of ownership called cooperative ownership. The lawyer said it couldn't be done.

"I know it can be done," I told him. I knew principles; I knew the underlying principles. I wrote what was called the first proprietary lease ever written. The lawyer said it was sound law. Of course it was sound law; it came from the Source. *I knew it.*

If You Want To Do Anything, Start Doing It

I always adopted that slogan of mine that "if you want to do anything, start doing it." Start at once doing the thing you wish to do *with full awareness and full comprehension that there is nothing that can stop you from doing it.* If you desire to do it, write that desire upon your heart and take it to sleep with you. If the answer is given you in the morning that says go ahead and do it, *that means the power of God is there.* With that full knowledge I would start doing it and *I knew before I started that I would succeed.* I say write that question upon your heart because I had begun to learn that the nights were more important than the days.

I have been asked many times to tell what the nights mean and what happens during sleep when the body is supposedly unconscious and wasting time. To the best of my ability I have tried to put that into words. The night is the time for *knowing;* the day is the time for acting. Our bodies are not active during the night; they are active during the day.

Our minds are not busy during the day conceiving because they are busy acting in the physical world. Therefore we haven't time to give to inspiration, to *knowing,* unless we take ourselves away from everything and lose ourselves in meditation.

My meditations were in the night when my body was asleep. Consciousness is not what you think it is. You think that when you stop thinking or are asleep that you are unconscious. *There is no such thing as a state of unconsciousness.* When the electric voltage of the body is lowered so that the electric current flowing through it isn't so strong as to keep you in a state of what you call wakefulness, you sink into slumber when night comes simply because your body has fatigued and is in the opposite cycle of its day, one part of it being the positive and the other the negative part of the cycle—just as with the planet, the day side being the positive side and the night the negative or expansive side.

The violets in the meadow fold up at night and the cattle lie down. Everything *seemingly* goes to sleep because the electric force that winds matter up and gives it what we call *the expression of life* lowers its voltage. Your body is likewise lowered in voltage so the electric current will not operate sufficiently to arouse those countless millions of little memories that you have photographed on your brain. When those little photographic images or records of events and things that you have observed are no longer functioning, you then become *unaware* of physical existence. I won't say you stop thinking because very few people think at all. They are but *electrically aware* of things, and so we unreel those electrically-photographed memories upon our brain and use them over and over again automatically. We call that thinking but it isn't thinking at all. It is an electrical awareness of an electrical existence and nothing more. It makes people aware of sensation. *Thinking is an extension of the Mind itself. Thinking is an electric extension in light of the knowing-Mind, extending that knowledge to waves of light and setting them in motion to express the ideas that are in the stillness.*

Consciousness Is A Glorious Awareness of Divine Being

Consciousness is not thinking. The awareness of consciousness in one who has lived in the God universe for a long time is an ecstatic and glorious awareness of Divine Being. It never leaves one night or day unless one has disobeyed and broken some law that makes it impossible for the Mind to be freed from the body. But if the body is normal and comfortable so that it can sleep, the Mind can be freed from the body. The Mind will go on and work for you and do just what you want it to do. It will give you that part of the whole idea which you are asking for, for your use the next day.

So I found during those years that what I wished to know in order to put into action the next day, I asked for when I went to sleep, and I had that knowledge when I awoke. I did not have to waste time the next day taking that idea apart bit by bit and putting it into motion. By *taking that idea apart* I mean this: in consciousness you conceive ideas as a whole. The whole idea comes to you in a flash, but it may take ten years to work it out by experimentation in laboratories or by the countless effort of putting into motion the different elements of matter, and by experimenting with all sorts of things to give you what you conceived as a whole in that flash of time, that flash of timelessness. It may take ten years for you to pick it apart by thinking out your *knowing.*

So the *knowing* is the *spiritual* part of life, and living in the *knowing* universe is what makes me different from other people. And the longer I lived in it and the more I worked in it, the more I was aware that I was being prepared for something great, something indefinite, gradually getting more force, gradually coming to a head, gradually feeling its way toward something very definite as each May came. This wonderful ecstasy of the Light came to glorify those twelve or fourteen days each year.

My Indescribable Experience In 1921

Then came the great experience in 1921. I was totally unaware that it would be different from anything else, but it was so utterly different! It was an experience which is so indescribable that I am not even going to attempt to do it. It is a very dangerous thing to go through because I doubt if very many could even recover from it. I doubt if I would have been willing to come back into the physical world if I hadn't had the Message, the command that I received.

The purpose for which I had been prepared all my life was so specific that I <u>had</u> to come back.

And even then it took three months to be willing to come back to a world which seemed so coarse and so terrible. Those thirty-nine days and nights were of great ecstasy in which the body and consciousness were practically severed. I was aware of my body, yes, like an instrument that we need to pick up and use when we want . But it didn't seem to be <u>me</u>. I had control of it just as I could pick up a pen to write with but I felt my body was detached from me. I felt when it was asleep that it was off on a shelf somewhere and I was glad of it. The more I was freed of it, the happier I was and the more ecstatic.

Of course the family was worried and, naturally, friends were worried, too, and wanted to take me on an ocean voyage and all sorts of things.

Example of Handwriting during my period
of Illumination in 1921

Papers Everywhere;
The Divine Iliad *in Parts*

Finally, after the doctors examined me and advised my wife to leave me alone, everyone did, and I was left alone. There were papers everywhere. *The Divine Iliad* was in parts everywhere, fragments of it, connected and disconnected. At first my handwriting was so illegible, going uphill and downhill, shaking and quaking, that afterward I could hardly decipher what I had written on those papers. And then I commanded my body to write perfectly, and I wrote like a school child in plain script, perfectly legible.

In those thirty-nine days and nights God spoke to me continuously in the language of Light which I knew as well as I know the English language that I am speaking to you now. It had a meaning, a vital meaning, a meaning fraught with the safety of the whole human race. It necessitated the uplift of the whole human race with new comprehension of this New Age.

The seed of that new comprehension for the uplift of the human race was mine to sow in the minds of ten men who would again reach out to ten more men, and another ten, and another ten until there would be legions. And the legions would sow the seed of Love to offset the seeds of hate and fear and greed that have brought us to the terrible impasse that we have been in, the old order where fear and hatred were abroad in the land, together with greed and selfishness — nation robbing nation, nation killing nation. ***That order must cease.***

It was then made known to me in 1921 that the first crop of the harvest that we had been reaping in the war was not finished. We had not been chastened sufficiently. The whole world would be drenched in blood and agony. All of that carnage will have ceased by 1946 and by that day I must be ready to begin to tell you and you and you what I am now telling you. I didn't even have the capacity of telling it in words. I had to prepare for it. I did not have the oratorical ability to tell it. God said I would have it and I must have it and I must prepare for it. And I knew I would, and I have. I have taken that responsibility upon myself and am asking you to take upon yourselves the responsibility of spreading this Message to all the world.

The Divine Iliad

I quote my instructions from *The Divine Iliad:*

It has been commanded of me to turn man's eyes away from his jungle, to tell him to look upon the face of the Lord, and know God's ecstasy in him. These are the words of the Lord. Hear thou them through me:

"The world of man is decadent. Go thou and resurrect it in my name.

"The beauty of My balanced thinking has man buried in his dank tombs and set ugliness in the images of man's earth thinking as idols for his worshiping.

"Man-might is he placing before Omnipotence in Me.

"Love is he seeking to crucify to deify brutality.

"Barbarity of his own inviting is e'en now crossing his horizon to crush him who would exalt it.

"The seeds of hate is he sowing for the babel of many tongues to multiply.

"I am a patient God. All men will come to Me in due time, but the agony of awaiting that day shall be theirs alone.

"And that day shall not come until man himself shall cleansed himself from his own unbalanced thinking.

"Prepare thou, therefore, My messenger to the Cosmic Age of ecstatic man, which is now in the deep dark before its dawning, and be thou ready for thine appointed day when man's own chastening shall awaken him in Me.

"Seven years hast thou to prepare for thy first beginning to manifest thy messengership to man. Guard well thy knowing, and herald not thy messengership for these first seven years of thy preparing.

"Then shall all the world begin to reap the harvest of self-inflicted suffering sown by his own hands in the seed of his unbalanced thinking.

"And the period of man's self cleansing shall be another three sevens of years added to the seven of thy novitiate years.

"And thine appointed day shall be in the eighteenth year of those three sevens, and be thou ready for that day, for thou shalt know no rest in worthily preparing to fulfill thine appointed task.

"Before that day of man's rebirth in Me his self-made way of earth will be deep strewn

with the ashes of his earth-planned tower of
self-might, denying Me in him.

"Untold suffering shall await him in the blood-
drenched road which leads toward the jungle
of his own seeking.

"Anguish will be his lot, and there will be
weeping in every home.

"And many who see such agony in man will
say to thee that a God of love cannot be if man
be son of God, and God the loving Father-
Mother of all men.

"But I say to thee, all men are one. The
thinking of one is the thinking of all, and so
shall the world-harvest be that which was
sown in the seed of world-thinking. Man's
world is the sum total of man's thinking. It is
what all world-thinking makes it.

"If love be in the world hate cannot also be.

"In the early days of this cycle My messenger of that day said: 'Love thy brother as thyself,' but man has not yet faintly comprehended its meaning.

"I now say more, for man is not now so new, and can well comprehend My meaning after the coming carnage by man shall have spent its furies, as the calm of earth's storms always follows those storms.

"These words I now say for newly comprehending man of his new cycle.

"Love ye one another all men, for ye are one in Me.

"Whatsoe'er you do to one in Me ye do to all; for all are one in Me.

"Love thy brother as thyself. Serve thy brother before thyself. Lift high thy brother, lift him to high pinnacles, for thy brother is thyself.

"For of a verity, I say, love of self, or a nation of selves, turns neighbor against neighbor and nation against nation. Self-love breeds hate and sows its seed in all the winds to blow where'er it will. Wherefore say I, love of neighbor by neighbor, and nation by nation, unites all men as one.

"Serve first thy brother. Hurt first thyself rather than thy neighbor. Gain naught from him unbalanced by thy giving. Protect thou the weak with thy strength, for if thou use thy strength against him his weakness will prevail against thee, and thy strength will avail thee naught.

"Such is My decree which thou well knowest in the inviolate workings of My law which holds balance in all creating things. See thou that man well knows this principle as the foundation of his new day."

*   *   *

I have herein given you parts of the unpublished sections of *The Message* which specifically instructs me in quite some detail as to the very manner and method of its delivery, as well as its time for delivery, yes, and even as to my failings as a man of earth manifesting God as a man of earth.

The Most Important Fact of Your Life

I have given you these instructions for the express purpose of bringing deeply home to you the most important—even though hardly believable—fact of your life. *This fact is that if you know God in you—not just abstractly believing it with some slight reservations — and work knowingly with God, your life will be the highest of the high, forever knowing the peace which passeth understanding, and your achievements will be mighty—for the divine YOU will be in them.*

The knowledge of your oneness with God is not possible of instant acceptance by any human in its fullness, as you would instantly accept the knowledge that two and two are four.

Such Illumination is too wonderful for quick unfoldment in man, for every cell in man's body cries out the selfhood of the body, and every sensation of man tells him of reality as being in the senses.

It is not a quick process to forget body and separability of bodies just by being told about it, even though you believe it. *Your body is the high hurdle which you must surmount in order to know your divinity.*

This story of my Illumination will help you to realize that you can put aside your body at will **— to a greater or lesser extent —** and know your divinity to the extent that you can put your body aside.

Now, as an answer to those who have asked me how in the world can knowledge be acquired in that way—I mean definite, specific knowledge, not abstractions, but "How can you make charts of the chemical elements or the heavens? How can you write a chemistry hundreds of years beyond your day without studying it from books?"

Well, it wasn't in books anyway. If I had gone to books, how could I have gotten it when it wasn't there? Everything that is in books is acquired bit by bit by men and put in books as they think they see it.

The Physical Universe—An Illusion Of Motion

This physical universe *is an illusion of motion.* The railroad tracks *seem* to meet upon the horizon. That is an illusion of perspective which only fools the artist. It doesn't have anything to do with chemistry or science. The illusion goes on down through the whole universe. The illusion of motion deceives everyone so that profound laws have been written by scientists which don't have the slightest foundation of truth in them, much less the very fundamental laws that I could see behind the scenes. When I came back I bought textbooks to find out the names of that which I knew in space in the universe in another way as zero – one–two–three–four–zero–four–three–two— one–and back to zero. That is all I needed to know. And the names of those–one–two–three– four, etc., are in text books: lithium, beryllium, boron, carbon, nitrogen, oxygen, fluorine, one series of elements after another. But to me they were always one–two–three–four–zero–four– three–two–one–zero–in everything, whether that was the octave spectrum of color or the octave on the piano. Every expression of motion is in the octave wave and I knew the wave. *And in the wave is the secret of creation and I had that. I knew it in a timeless flash.*

And God said to me, *"There will be those who will question. There will be those who doubt. There will be those who crucify you. I give to thee a sign by which thou canst prove thyself.*

Thou who has never known a chemist's laboratory shall know chemistry beyond men. To thee all chemists will come for knowledge of the Light. Thou who has never known the stars save with thine adoring eyes shall know the stars beyond all men. All astronomers will come to thee for the new mappings of the universe of the stars which thou shalt give to them. To thee who to study mathematics was a dreary thing, shall I give the master key to mathematics. To thee all mathematicians will come for knowledge of the key to motion and the curvature of space."

And one thing after another like that—I'm trying to recall the exact words from *The Divine Iliad*—that was to be a sign whereby I could prove my right to speak with authority. And the signs never failed. And with them came the admonition that I should keep perfectly quiet and not herald my messengership for seven years, but should prepare for the first rehearsal of it by "thy written word."

THE FOUR FREEDOMS
Walter Russell - Sculptor

Freedom From Fear
Freedom From Want
Freedom of Speech
Freedom of Religion

"The four freedoms of common humanity are as much elements of man's needs as air and sunlight, bread and salt. Deprive him of all these freedoms and he dies–deprive him of a part of them and a part of him withers. Give them to him in full and abundant measure and he will cross the threshold of a new age, the greatest age of man. These freedoms are the rights of men of every creed and every race, wherever they live. This is their heritage, long withheld."

Franklin D. Roosevelt

I, as a sculptor, followed the suggestion of the President and gave this symbol of the Four Freedoms – that of four angels with upraised wings – a visual form in order that the world might better visualize the standard which they must henceforth attain.

W.R.

My First Book

So I wrote a book in those seven years and gave it to the world. Science laughed at it, scoffed at it, threw it in the wastebasket. And then gradually discovered that what I had written was so and men took those ideas as their own. Two Nobel prizes have been given for ideas that were in that book. A prominent scientist wrote to *The New York Sun* remonstrating why scientists should take those ideas of mine and put them out as their own and not give me credit for them. He remonstrated with me, also, for not insisting upon having the credit.

"It makes no difference to me whatsoever," I told him, "so long as those ideas are brought into the world. They will come back to their source some day and it will be known where they came from. That is all I want. I want those ideas to go out into the world and begin to take effect."

Gradually they did take effect. The head of the

physics department of one of the great universities resigned his position because he could not teach there any longer. He had been a private pupil of mine for months and he said he could never go back and teach, even though he had a family and was paying installments on a house, so it was a serious thing for him to give up a well-paying position. He set up a chemist's laboratory of his own. He is a consulting chemist now and has made three times his former salary the first year. He is making more than five times that now.

For months, I had lunch with him every Tuesday at the Lotus Club in New York. He talked to me each Tuesday until he got to know my language.

So that started out with one physicist who knew, then another, and then another and another. And then my book became accepted and letters were published in the newspapers, letters that were for it as well as against it. The Science Editor of *The Associated Press* then wrote another letter stating that my observations and my writings should be studied because it may be that I had a new key to things.

A well-known physicist wrote to *The New York Times* and said that I had better go back to my easel, that I was a good painter but I was blaspheming Newton and Kepler by questioning their laws. *The New York Times* let me answer that in the same column, and my answer was so convincing to this man that he invited me to lunch. At the luncheon table he told me that he was about to give up upon a problem that he had been working on for months. He was about to give it up because he could no longer hope to solve it.

I said, " What is it? Tell me. Perhaps I can help you."

It was very difficult for him to even be polite. "If I can't solve it," he said, "how in the world can you pretend to do it? I can't take you into my laboratory."

"I don't want to go into your laboratory. Tell me your problem."

And he did. There at the luncheon table I solved the problem for him. I said, "You are looking on the wrong side of the fence for the stabilizer you need." Arsenic and bismuth and all those negative elements, according to his theory, was where he would find that which he was looking for.

I said, "Two elements on the positive side will do it, either aluminum or boron. If you want conductivity, use aluminum. If you want brittleness, use boron."

"I want conductivity," he answered.

And he found that aluminum did it. He called me up at two o'clock in the morning and told me so and thanked me. And then he wrote a long letter of apology to *The New York Times* and gradually that specific new knowledge that I had went far, far beyond the science of that day and even that of this day. I haven't begun to breathe all of it yet, not even begun. A little at a time only. And that got me a Doctor's Degree of Science—a man who had never been in a university getting a Doctor's Degree of Science!

Then I was elected president of *The Society of Arts and Sciences,* a very dignified position with a very dignified society founded by Herbert Spencer over fifty years before.

Since then I have come to know the greatest scientists in the world. I gave lectures there and in universities and at engineers' clubs. When a medal was bestowed on Thomas Edison I gave a scientific lecture and always went a little bit farther than what they knew; just enough to set them talking. And they respected me because so many things had come true.

Hydrogen—Not Number One Element

Then the great time came when I was given an

interview by one of the greatest chemists of California. I gave my lecture on hydrogen to four hundred of the most distinguished scientists in the world. One more little idea, one step in breaking down the old suppositions, the old patterns, the old designs that believed that hydrogen was the Number One element in the series when there were numerous others preceding it that they didn't know anything about.

They also thought that hydrogen was a single element. I told them there were six other full tone elements in it, a whole octave in it; that it was a complex element. They couldn't believe it. But they went testing in their laboratories. They took it apart. They called those other elements isotopes. Isotopes are supposedly split tones like the black notes between two white notes on the piano. You split a tone into a half tone. In chemistry they call that an isotope.

"They're not isotopes," I told them. "They are full toned elements of that octave."

"Oh, but they have to be isotopes," they insisted. "We have no place in our table of the elements for them otherwise. It throws out all of our theories on the structure of the atom."

I said, "You might just as well throw them out now because you will eventually."

In that lecture I told them they could have a different kind of water, that if oxygen united with one of those so-called isotopes of hydrogen, we would have a water that would be intensely valuable in future chemical life. So heavy water was discovered from that, and heavy water is the basis of the atomic bomb.

In the charts that I have made, the two elements that have been discovered very recently, neptunium and plutonium, constitute the basis for the atom bomb. Those two elements were in my charts twenty years ago. Long before they were discovered they were in my charts. And beside them, in brackets, I had this notation: "If these two elements are ever discovered, the pressure of this planet cannot hold them together."

Beside those two, there were thirteen others that I didn't name that were yet to be discovered. They have discovered one of those since. How did I know? Surely I didn't get it from books. The only answer is that God told me. That is the only answer. *I knew it because all knowledge exists, and we can have it for the asking.*

All of that was merely a sign, a sign by means of which I could prove myself as an authority, as a messenger sent by God to do His bidding. All of my life is a sign, *a demonstration that power gained from the Source was possible,* and not from a manifestation of the Source. As Glenn Clark said in his little book that I have lived five lives, it is because it's just as easy for me to live five lives as it is for you to live one. And it is just as easy for you to multiply yourself by five or ten as it is for me to have multiplied myself in that same way.

This New Civilization Must Live In a Universe of **Knowing**

I say this new civilization must stop depending solely upon the sensed universe of thinking and manifesting a borrowed power. It must live in the universe of knowing and *know that from the Source, and believe it and make use of it.* The purpose is for the saving of the whole human race. In *The Divine Iliad* it was given me to know that civilization would be self-destroyed unless it was met by this opposing seed of Love that must be planted in order to draw out the seeds of hate and fear that are abroad in the land. In the words of the *Divine Iliad*:

> *"If love be in the world,*
> *hate cannot also be."*

The world has not yet come to that positive aspect of life because we are still so near the jungle, so near that we haven't cast off the fears and hatreds and greeds of the jungle. As soon as we got out of our animal existence and became aware of material things, a greed developed in us for material things, greed and selfishness for possessions, material possessions, things of earth, things that have no meaning, things that we cannot take with us. *And we pay for those things with our lives.*

We pay for them with a dozen incarnations, perhaps, to balance them, instead of balancing our lives now with the qualities and values of Heaven instead of those of earth. We are just wasting our lives. I have told you this, as I say, reluctantly, but again joyously because if my life can be an example, and if the way I have received my education can be an example to you, I encourage you to emulate it. If it helps to deliver the Message which I am here to deliver, I am glad to give it.

If you really want to know much more about this than I have had time to tell you, I would say go and get a book published by E. P. Dutton and Company, written by Richard Maurice

Bucke, the title of which is *Cosmic Consciousness.* Richard Maurice Bucke had a touch of cosmic consciousness himself, and it so transformed him that he gave the rest of his life to analyzing the symptoms of it and studying it all down through history, studying all the cases he could find. He found thirty-seven, some who just had a bit of it, and one only who had complete cosmic consciousness, Jesus the Nazarene. A few had it very deeply, but perhaps there were not more than three or four or five in all history.

If some of you do not believe it possible, I merely point to the evidence of it in my life and in my works and the things I shall prove to you as I go along. And if you put them into effect yourself, *you will find that God is the only reality in the universe;* that all we have to consider and all we have to know is *Light* — the Light at the center of us and the two lights of motion which is *thinking* from the Spirit within us. Mind and Mind-thinking; Creator and Creation; Creator and those who are co-

Creating with God or alone by themselves. I choose to be co-Creator with God and stand upon that fulcrum.

If you choose to depend entirely upon yourself, you will be way behind in your class for the few hundred thousand years that you still have to go on that long journey to the mountain top. But I'm not concerned about even ten thousand years; I'm concerned about these next seven years.

This messenger of the Light must have hundreds of thousands of messengers of the Light to spread this new comprehension lest man destroy himself and begin all over again in the dark ages, a deeper and longer dark ages than we have ever known before.

Franklin D. Roosevelt,
Walter Russell, Sculptor

WHO IS
WALTER RUSSELL?

Internationally distinguished
**Sculptor - Painter - Author - Architect -
Composer - Philosopher - Scientist**

Familiarly known as -
> The most versatile man in America
> The modern Leonardo
> The man who tapped the secrets of the
> universe.

*   *   *

He believed that every man has unlimited power to do whatever he desires to do and that whatever he does he should excel in it.

> Compiled in part from *Who's Who in America* and from Glenn Clark's story of Walter Russell's life in *The Man Who Tapped The Secrets of The Universe.*

First Years

Born in Boston May 19, 1871. Attended village school until nearly ten, then put to work as a cash boy because of family reverses.

Musician and Composer - 1884 to 1889

Church organist and music teacher from age thirteen to nineteen. A natural musician, never having studied music, he gave piano recitals at ten years of age. Composed about a hundred musical themes before age nineteen. Paderewski accidently heard him play and urged him to become a musician, and liked one composition so much that he had it written into manuscript form thirty years later after requesting Russell to play it at a distinguished musical gathering.

Illustrator - 1889 to 1898

First illustrated Mark Twain's magazines published by D. Lothrup. Became Mark Twain's life-long friend and, later, official sculptor. Became Art Editor of Collier's, then resigned to represent Collier's and Century Magazines in the Spanish-American War. While there he first met President Theodore Roosevelt for whom he later became official painter.

Painter - from 1898

First painted his now famous allegory *The Might of Ages* which won him international distinction and citations, honorable mentions and medals from eleven European countries; and the personal approval of King Alphonso of Spain and King Albert of Belgium (who later visited him at his New York Studio).

As a portrait painter he specialized in children's portraits for many years, including children of President Theodore Roosevelt, Governor Oliver Ames of Massachusetts, and other notable families all over the country.

In 1903 the *Ladies Home Journal* commissioned him to select and paint the twelve most beautiful childen in America. In 1914 he ceased painting children and painted many portraits of notables, including Sir Thomas Lipton, Archbishop Corrigan, Thomas A. Edison, Clayton Sedgewick Cooper, Bishop Alexander Garrett, Hudson Maxim, and many others.

Architect - 1900 to 1926

Designed, financed and erected the famous West 67th Street Studio Colony for artists, including the famous Hotel des Artistes — also many other New York buildings such as the first Hotel Pierre at 48th and Park, Alwyn Court, and the West 81st and West 86th Street Studio buildings. Designed many buildings for Florida, including two whole civic centers.

Sculptor - from 1927

At age of 56, never having touched sculpture, was commissioned by the Edison

Company to make a bust of Thomas A. Edison which has become the official bust. Since then, he has executed about ninety sculptural pieces, including the following four monuments:

> *The Mark Twain Memorial*
> (proclaimed his masterpiece)
> *The Charles Goodyear Memorial*
> *The Four Freedoms,* and
> *The Christ of the Blue Ridge.*

Other portrait busts and bas reliefs include those of Cass Gilbert, Victor Herbert, Ossip Gabrilowitsch, John Phillip Sousa, George Gershwin, Charles Goodyear, Colette D'Arville, Sir Thomas Lipton, Colin Kelly, Thomas Watson, General MacArthur, Cardinal Farley, Franklin Roosevelt, Dr. H. H. Sheldon, and others.

Scientist

In 1926 he announced to the scientific world a complete and consistent plan for the constitution of matter to replace the present inconsistent one. He announced that the then *seemingly* complete Mendeleef table of elements was incomplete, and gave to the world new and complete charts of nine octaves to replace the five-octave Mendeleef chart. Included in his charts were the hydrogen "isotopes" which led to the discovery of heavy water three years later—and the six transuranium elements which gave atomic energy to the world thirteen years later. Science has long resisted the Russell cosmogony for the acceptance by science would mean the complete overthrow of the present cosmogony, yet the Russell cosmogony is slowly seeping into conventional science, especially in industry and with engineers.

He became President of the *Society of Arts and Sciences* in 1927 and held that post for seven years. During that time he conferred medals of honor to such persons in the arts and sciences as Thomas A. Edison, Robert A. Millikan, A. A. Michaelson, Harlow Shapley, John Philip Sousa, Cass Gilbert, Eve Le Gallienne and many others.

For his new chemical charts and his work on hydrogen, a Doctor of Science Degree was conferred on him by the American Academy of Sciences which was chartered as a university with power to give degrees earned by work performed of a nature which would benefit mankind.

Sports

Won national championship in figure-skating at the age of forty-four and held it for four years. Introduced figure-skating in New York and gave first two skating carnivals in Madison Square Garden. Won three first prizes at sixty-nine. Owned a stable of Arabian and Clay Arabian horses. Trained stallions for high school and saddle. Known as one of the best horsemen in America.

Philosopher and Lecturer

Has lectured upon the philosophy of life for many years. For twelve years was retained by International Business Machines Corporation to lecture to directors and sales force upon new ethical principles for business which placed **service first** ahead of **sales first.** Together with his philosopher wife, Lao Russell, had made many coast-to-coast lecture tours. They have also written a one-year Home Study Course in *Universal Law, Natural Science and Living Philosophy* which has already girdled the world, in addition to their numerous other books.

The Walter Russell Foundation - 1948

Lao Russell established this Foundation as a permanent memorial to her husband and as a headquarters for their teachings. It became *The University of Science and Philosophy* in 1957. It is located on top of Mount Afton in Virginia and consisted of an estate of 629 acres upon which an Italian Renaissance marble palace and sculptured gardens had been erected by wealthy Southerners at a cost of many millions. In this palace are gathered together many of Walter Russell's works in painting and sculpture, and in the gardens are The Four Freedoms and The Christ of the Blue Ridge.

THE FOUR FREEDOMS

The first is *freedom of speech and expression* – everywhere in the world.

The second is *freedom of every person to worship God in his own way* – everywhere in the world.

The third is *freedom from want* – which, translated into world terms, means economic understandings which will secure to every nation a healthy peacetime life for its inhabitants – everywhere in the world.

The fourth is *freedom from fear* – which, translated into world terms, means a world-wide reduction of armaments to such a point and in such a thorough fashion that no nation will be in a position to commit an act of physical aggression against any neighbor anywhere in the world.

WALTER RUSSELL
Author of

The Secret of Light
The Message of the Divine Iliad - Vol. I
The Message of the Divine Iliad - Vol. II
A New Concept of the Universe
The Quest of The Grail
The Electric Nature of the Universe
The Sculptor Searches for Mark Twain's Immortality
The Fifth Kingdom Man
The Dawn of a New Day in Human Relations
The Immortality of Man

WALTER and LAO RUSSELL
Co-Authors of

Home Study Course in *Universal Law, Natural Science
and Living Philosophy*
Scientific Answer to Human Relations
Atomic Suicide?

LAO RUSSELL
Author of

God Will Work Under You But Not For You
Love—A Scientific & Living Philosophy of Love and Sex
Why You Cannot Die!—Reincarnation Explained

*For catalog on additional books and teachings by
Walter and Lao Russell, please write or phone:*

The University of Science and Philosophy
P.O. Box 520
Waynesboro, Virginia 22980
(800) 882-LOVE (5683) Book Orders
www.philosophy.org